Financial Intelligence

A simple money mentality approach to help you reach financial independence

Anthony L. Thomas and Bartholomew O. Utazi

Copyright © 2024 - Anthony L. Thomas and Bartholomew O. Utazi All rights reserved.

The content contained within this book may not be reproduced, duplicated, or transmitted without direct written permission from the authors or the publisher. This book is copyright protected. This book is only for personal use. You cannot amend, distribute, sell, use, quote, paraphrase any part, or the content within this book, without the consent of the authors or publisher.

Disclaimer Notice:

Please note the information contained within this document is for educational and entertainment purposes only. All effort has been executed to present accurate, up-to-date, and reliable, complete information. However, no warranties of any kind are declared or implied. Readers acknowledge that the author is not engaged in rendering legal, financial, medical, or professional advice. The content within this book has been derived from various sources. Please consult a licensed professional before attempting any techniques outlined in this book. Under no circumstances will any blame or legal responsibility be held against the publisher, or author, for any damages, reparation, or monetary loss due to the information contained within this book. Either directly or indirectly. You are responsible for your own choices, actions, and results.

Table of contents

Introduction 7
Chapter 1 10
What is Financial Intelligence? 10
Important Elements of Financial Intelligence and How to Apply Them 10
Chapter 2 14
Setting up Your Financial Mindset 14
What Is Money Mindset? 16
How Did You Develop Your Money Mindset? 18
    Important pointers for developing a good money perspective 18
Chapter 3 24
You can work two hours for yourself after eight hours of work for someone else 24
How to Get an Additional Two Hours Every Day 24
Introducing the Two-Hour Rule 27
Chapter 4 29
Expert Budgeting 29
Expert Budgeting Techniques 29
Chapter 5 33
Financial Leverage 33
What Does Financial Leverage Mean? 33
Comprehending Financial Leverage 33
How to Calculate Your Leverage Amount 34
Benefits and Drawbacks of Financial Leverage 38
    Benefits 38
    Drawbacks 38
    Leverage Pros 39
    Cons 39
Chapter 6 41
Make Financial Decisions Automatically 41
    Streamline Your Budget and Bills 41
    Automate Your Savings and Banking 44
    Automate Your Financial and Investing Objectives 46
    Things Not to Automate 48
Chapter 7 50
Net Worth Factor 50
Your Net Worth: What Is It? 50
    How Your Net Worth Is Determined 51
Chapter 8 55
Avoiding needless taxes 55
    Tax Evasion vs. Tax Avoidance 55
Chapter 9 63
Wise management of time 63

    Time Management Strategies to Increase Your Income 63
    The advantages of devoting time to your finances 68
    Consequences of Ineffective Time Management 70
Chapter 10 71
Checklist for Financial Freedom 71
What Is Financial Freedom? 71
    How may one achieve financial independence? 71
Conclusion 77
REFERENCES 79

Introduction

Let us establish the expectations up front before we get started. First off, while I do invest and encourage you to do the same, this book is not about making financial decisions. Furthermore, this is not a sophisticated financial book filled with jargon that most readers will find confusing. Nor will they even tell you "how to become rich in 3 days" or offer you magic tricks. The subject matter of this book is far more significant. I advise you to devote all of your time, money, and energy to yourself. How come? Yes, make the most of everything at your disposal to improve yourself. You'll gain more information, expand your network, love your profession, and have more time to fortify your relationships in addition to achieving greater outcomes. This book also focuses on developing an open mind to consider and weigh the several significant facets of your financial life. Your life should, for instance, strike a balance between your relationships, career, family, health, spirituality, and emotional well-being.

Similarly, if you wish to improve your financial intelligence, you also need to maintain a healthy balance in your financial life. If all you think about is making money and you don't know how to keep it, you can't expect to be wealthy. Even if you are the greatest stock picker in the world, losing everything in a divorce still doesn't matter. Even if you created a sound budget and kept track of every dollar you spent, it won't help if you allow Uncle Sam to siphon out a sizable portion of your savings at tax time. We refer to that as being "pound foolish, penny wise." Additionally, working for more than 40 years at a job you detest just to be able to retire doesn't make you happy. Think beyond; you are worthy of more.

This book will walk you through the process of understanding your financial situation and making improvements as you go.

This book will help you make the move from a typical full-time job that everyone hates to starting your dream business that nobody wants to start on Monday.

It's okay if you are an exception and genuinely like what you do. But since everyone needs a balanced financial life, you will also gain from this book. The best guidelines to improve your financial intelligence are provided in this book. Why does that matter? Since knowledge, not wealth, is the solution to issues, No matter how much money you make, if you don't know what to do with it, you will find a way to waste it. That is also the idea behind filling a water container. If the amount of liquid you can pour is restricted, you won't be able to hold onto more liquid unless you enlarge your container. With money, it works the same way. Your current financial situation is a direct reflection of your mental state. Thus, in order to increase your income, you must first increase your knowledge, intelligence, and skill set. When you do this, your income will increase on its own. Your thinking determines how successful you are.

Some people are just naturally prudent and frugal with their money when it comes to spending, including myself in the past. I am aware that it is a process and that things take time to alter. Seeing individuals spend money on things they do not need instead of the things they need most, however, is upsetting. They're making poor financial decisions, whether it's because they want to "keep up with the Joneses" or just show off how much money they make. Don't feel bad if you have used your money improperly in the past. Remorse for your decisions makes you stronger and helps you make fewer mistakes in the future. Because habits are hard to break, most people who make mistakes will never change. That ought to make one feel guilty. It is a sign that you don't want to better yourself when you don't want to change your behaviors. Fortunately, if you're reading this book, you're open to trying new things or at least changing your routines.

Next thing to do

It's time to make a decision now. Would you like to find yourself in similar precarious financial situations that you have experienced? Will you keep making dubious financial choices even after realizing that they might be a series of serious errors? Alternatively, would you like to enhance your financial intelligence? Something that you can consistently get passive revenue from and a mechanism that will continue to automate your savings and investments for years to come.

This book will be of great assistance to you if that is your desire. Every chapter ends with action steps. So, adhere to the instructions we've given.

If you don't do something, nothing in this book will work. Making the commitment to live a financially wise life is the first thing you should do right now. Say that out loud now. Do you now have that resolved?

Alright. Now let's turn the page and start.

Chapter 1

What is Financial Intelligence?

The capacity to comprehend and efficiently handle one's financial matters is known as financial intelligence. Regardless of income level, financial intelligence is the capacity to comprehend and efficiently manage your resources. It entails managing debt, investing for the future, and learning how to make wise financial decisions. A lack of financial literacy can result in a multitude of dangers, including the accumulation of unmanageable debt loads, bankruptcy, or other unfavorable outcomes. It entails a blend of abilities, dispositions, and information that empower people to make wise choices regarding their financial resources, both now and down the road.

Important Elements of Financial Intelligence and How to Apply Them

Effective money management requires a few fundamental elements of financial understanding. It does, however, require time and work to incorporate these elements into your daily life, but the investment will eventually pay off. These elements consist of:

Knowledge of finances

The basis of financial intelligence is financial literacy. It entails comprehending financial ideas, including debt management, investing, saving, and budgeting. It is hard to manage your money wisely and make educated financial decisions if you lack financial literacy. To become financially literate, one must first learn.

To increase your financial literacy, read books, go to seminars, and enroll in online courses. To keep up with the latest news and trends in money, follow financial gurus on social media or sign up for financial newsletters.

Additionally, there are a ton of free tools out there that can assist you in improving your financial knowledge, such as blogs, podcasts, and YouTube channels.

Setting a budget

Constructing a detailed plan that monitors your income and expenses and ranks your purchases according to your financial objectives—is the process of constructing a budget. You can take charge of your money, manage your resources wisely, and work toward your financial goals by creating a budget.

Finding places to minimize costs and making sure you have enough money to pay your bills and invest in your objectives are the cornerstones of budgeting. Our most recent posts have additional information about creating a budget.

Saving

Saving is still a crucial part of sound financial management. It entails putting money aside for investments, short- and long-term objectives, emergencies, and retirement. You can make sure that you are ready for unforeseen expenses by making regular savings. You should think about automating your savings because it will help you develop discipline. Bitnob provides automated bitcoin savings if you're interested in storing money in digital currencies. You have the option to schedule your savings to run on a daily, weekly, or monthly basis.

Making Investments

Another crucial component of accumulating wealth and reaching financial freedom is investing. It describes the process of distributing or investing funds, assets, or cash into different acceptable chances with the hopes of earning a profit over a predetermined time frame.

By choosing appropriate assets, businesses, or financial instruments with the potential to grow in value or produce income, the investment seeks to raise or grow the initial sum of money.

But wise investments also entail picking the ideal asset to put money into. According to statistics and trends, Bitcoin is the asset that has performed the best over the past ten years. It is not necessary to start investing in Bitcoin with a large amount of wealth.

As you get started with bitcoin, you may apply the dollar cost averaging technique. Of course, you'll also need a platform that facilitates this investing process.

Debt Control

The act of eliminating debt and preventing new debt is known as debt management. It means avoiding debt with high interest rates and creating a repayment strategy. To reduce your interest rates, think about refinancing high-interest loans or consolidating your debt.

Financial planning

Financial planning involves creating and carrying out long-term financial plans that complement individual objectives and priorities.

Management of risks

Understanding and managing financial risks, such as loss of income, unanticipated expenses, and market volatility.

The skills needed for financial intelligence

Problem-solving and critical thinking: the capacity to assess possibilities, analyze financial data, and come to well-informed conclusions.

Collaboration and communication: the capacity to cooperate with others to accomplish financial objectives and to successfully convey financial information.

Organizing and arranging: the capacity to properly manage resources, set financial goals, and make financial plans.

Resilience and adaptability: the capacity to handle financial stress, overcome obstacles, and adjust to shifting financial conditions.

Chapter 2

Setting up Your Financial Mindset

The best approach to developing financially savvy behaviors is to establish a particular frame of mind. In this chapter, we'll be discussing precisely that. For instance, if your mentality encourages you to continue spending money, you cannot be financially savvy. Furthermore, you will never be financially successful if you hold grudges against yourself for past financial transgressions. It is critical to adopt a mindset that enables you to view money from an alternative perspective. You should value it far more than the average person would. You should be in a better position to save money and take advantage of your financial situation if you can think outside the box.

We will discuss how to develop a money mindset and how to think about money. Furthermore, we'll teach you how to comprehend it from the beginning because we think that managing your money wisely will help you achieve financial success. This is the kind of thinking that has greatly benefited the wealthy. It's not as easy as pressing a button and behaving flawlessly to shift one's perspective. Undoubtedly, a lot of people have made financial mistakes, but giving up is not an option.

Examining our past errors in order to make better decisions going forward is not enjoyable. But in order to succeed, that's essential. You must examine your previous attitudes if you wish to make improvements in your business, relationships, budget, investments, negotiations, career, or spiritual life.

Essentially, enough said, our present findings are predicated on our prior experiences. Now let's get started.

All humans make errors. Since we are all humans, we have all erred financially in the past. I have, as well as you. Moving forward and taking measures to ensure that such mistakes don't happen again is the best course of action.

These errors could be minor or major. If you stay away from the tiny mistakes, they won't have a big impact on your life. However, this does not imply that you should continue saying them. These are errors, including overspending on unnecessary or undesired services or subscriptions, paying bank fees, holding onto undesirable things rather than returning them, going out to eat too frequently, not properly planning unaffordable vacations, and so on.

Inadequate time management can also be expensive since you could be creating something, learning something, or even just spending time with loved ones. Avoid sacrificing quality in favor of cost savings; this can be quite costly since it may leave you feeling unsatisfied with your purchases and may eventually lead to future overspending due to a distorted mindset. Additionally, a subpar product may persuade you to purchase a new one in order to satisfy your wants. The major errors that lead to debt are those that we make. They take a long time to get rid of, and they can leave us feeling hopeless. They also have additional effects on our lives, including emotional and interpersonal ones. Big mistakes include, but are not limited to, investing a sizable portion of your money in risky stocks, taking out a loan to invest in a failing company, buying a luxury car that you can no longer afford to pay for, and many more.

The above-mentioned examples are excellent places to start. It's likely that someone is lying to you if they have ever claimed they have never made a financial error in their lives. While you're about it, try not to think back on prior errors. Rather, make use of them as a teaching tool.

Even some of the most well-known individuals have erred financially. However, they weren't the type to give up and go away. Rather, they made the decision to start over from scratch and rebuild.

Pardon your financial errors

Right now, forgiving yourself for your financial errors is the wisest course of action. Recognize them, take what you can from them, and proceed. If not, you may find yourself prone to repeating the same errors. It is imperative that you never permit them to imprison you and prevent you from ever being able to escape. Having a strategy and sticking to it is the only way out of the situation. So, before reading this chapter further, consider your past failures and challenges. The greater your obstacles, the greater the lessons you have learned. Let's go on to understand your financial thinking now.

What Is Money Mindset?

A mindset is predicated on particular ideas and attitudes. A money mindset typically revolves around personal and business money. A preset set of beliefs about money is known as a financial mindset. Your individual collection of beliefs and perspectives around money is known as your money mindset. It influences the choices you make regarding handling, saving, and spending money.

Your financial mindset determines your way of thinking about money and affects the way you spend, save, and handle debt. It's your attitude toward money and your underlying thoughts about it.

This comprises:

What you believe you can and can't accomplish financially;

How much you believe you should be paid;

How you think you ought to handle your finances (spent, saved, shared);

How you think you ought to handle your debt;

Your capacity to develop your wealth;

Your general assurance regarding finances.

What mindsets and beliefs do you have regarding your money? For instance, you might be asking yourself, if you have a bad money perspective.

"How can I afford this? That is not something I am capable of."

"It is impossible for me to make more money."

"I wish I can purchase that. However, I don't have enough cash."

These are only poor illustrations of having a negative financial mindset. However, the following illustrations of a sound financial mindset stand in sharp contrast to the ones previously provided:

"I can reach my financial objectives. I will succeed, but it will take time."

"I'm able to purchase that. To obtain it, all I have to do is accumulate sufficient funds."

"Why should I evaluate myself against other people? With what I have, I'm content."

"My money is my own to spend however I wish. However, I have no problem saying no to purchases."

How Did You Develop Your Money Mindset?

Your daily surroundings and interactions with other people set the tone for how you approach money. If anything at all, what lessons regarding money did your parents impart to you? How was money managed in your childhood home? Did you see more optimism or negativity related to money? Families may find it taboo or sensitive to discuss money, but a lack of communication can allow the terrible financial cycle to pass down through the generations.

Recall that your parents' lack of understanding about money and their experiences growing up are not necessarily your responsibility. Your pals may also have different opinions on money as you get older. Their experiences may differ greatly from yours and may have a favorable or unfavorable effect on you. Additionally, your money perspective will be significantly influenced by your neighbors, the schools you attended, the area where you grew up, and, if you get married, your spouse.

Important pointers for developing a good money perspective

In order to assist you in developing a more positive financial mindset as you proceed on your path to achieving true riches, here are some pointers. Recall that you may attain success by altering your financial habits and thinking, regardless of your present financial circumstances.

1. Make the decision to succeed financially

In reality, becoming wealthy begins long before you open an account for investments or deposit money into a savings account.

It all begins with a seemingly insignificant but momentous decision.

It's making the decision that you will become wealthy, which in turn requires making the decision to trust the process and dedicate yourself to the path.

A tremendous mental lift comes from deciding (with complete conviction) that you are going to be wealthy. This is a result of your decision to convince yourself that you are capable of succeeding. You're not likely to put in the effort necessary to truly accumulate riches unless you firmly believe that you are capable of doing so.

2. Establish your principles in life

Once you've made the decision that you will become wealthy, you must ascertain why you desire this level of financial achievement. That entails figuring out your "why." Your "why" gives you a strong feeling of purpose and provides the necessary drive. As a matter of fact, having a "why" can enhance aspects of your life that are directly related to your level of happiness.

Why, therefore, do you wish to reduce your debt, save money, achieve financial success, become financially independent, etc.? Finding your "why" will be your greatest source of inspiration. In particular, on the days or throughout the seasons when your plans are not coming to pass.

3. Give up on norms and concentrate on what matters most to you

You have to do what works for you when it comes to accumulating wealth and improving your money attitude; it's crucial to avoid getting sucked into standards imposed by society. Additionally, since comparison is the thief of joy, you should refrain from doing so. Here we return to your "why."

If you wish to retire early, your notion of financial freedom may be $500,000, or it may be $1 million. Perhaps your only financial objective is to save up enough cash to go on an international backpacking trip. Whatever your objectives, keep your attention on your personal standards and what money means to you in regard to your life's ambitions.

4. Learn to live with your fears and your discomfort

Fear and anxiety are inevitable side effects of wanting to achieve something significant. There are the fears of failing, of change, and of the unknown. Furthermore, fear frequently has the power to completely paralyze you and overwhelm you.

particularly when you begin to imagine all the "what ifs" and "what nots" that surround hypothetical events that, more often than not, never come to pass.

The problem with fear, though, is that you really only have two options because it comes with the territory. Allowing it to keep you stuck is the first option. The second, and wiser, option is to accept fear as a necessary companion on the journey and to communicate with it. Looking back at all of your successes to date and the fears you overcame to get there might help you remember your "why" and conquer fear. You can absolutely overcome your present money-related worries if you can overcome those ones.

There is probably at least one thing you can do, no matter how minor, to combat every fear you may have. Are you worried, for instance, that you will always be in debt? To combat that dread, you can concentrate on paying off debt now or in the near future.

No matter how scary it may be, tell yourself repeatedly that you can accomplish this and concentrate on making tiny progress every day before you realize it, you'll have come a long way.

5. Show appreciation

One of the best exercises for improving your money attitude is to express thankfulness since it helps you to refocus your attention. When you are thankful, you give more thought to all the blessings you have received as well as the things you already have for which you are grateful.

Moreover, gratitude fosters contentment, which is essential for accumulating wealth. When you are happy with what you have, you are less inclined to spend money on things that won't necessarily satisfy you—you'll always be able to buy something new. Take advantage of our 30-day appreciation challenge to get started.

6. Use affirmations to change your perspective on money

It's really simple for negativity to seep into our thoughts. But you can counter those negative thoughts with positive ones! Including daily positive financial affirmations into your routine is another excellent way to start practicing a money attitude. Actually, research indicates that repeating positive affirmations can rewire your brain! Thus, adopting affirmations will enhance your perspective and provide you a sound financial mindset. For additional positive thinking, read our post on "55 Financial Affirmations You Should Tell Yourself" to put an end to your negative self-talk.

7. Try not to focus on your previous financial errors

It's time to quit punishing yourself for previous financial missteps. Why? Since the way to success is through failure! We've all made errors and experienced financial difficulties, but you can utilize them as opportunities to improve yourself. This involves enhancing your financial situation. Therefore, instead of focusing on your mistakes, use the lessons you learned from the past to create a financial strategy that will help you do better.

8. Give up constrictive money ideas

Another essential step in developing a healthy money mentality is letting go of limiting beliefs. Constraining ideas do exactly that—they confine you. If you put in the effort, you can succeed financially! Put some large, bold, and ambitious goals on paper and aim high.

Utilizing your daily affirmations is also beneficial for this reason. They will assist you in dispelling your outdated notions and establishing limitless new ones!

9. Take use of coaching and courses on money attitude

So, how can you change the way you think about money? Obtain instruction on your money mindset! The best part is that there is no financial obligation.

Free money mentality coaching calls with our mentors are available through Clever Girl Finance! In addition, we offer over 50 hours of archived replay films covering a broad range of financial subjects. We also provide more than thirty free financial courses and worksheets! A "how to transform your money mindset course" is included in our "Build a solid foundation" bundle to help you shift from having an abundance mindset to a scarcity mindset.

To give you the resources you need to succeed financially, we also offer entirely free courses on anything from investing to budgeting!

10. Use fin-fluencers to change your perspective on money

Getting motivated by fin-fluencers is a great approach to improve your perspective on money. They assist you in realizing that they, too, have erred financially so you won't have to live with regret or humiliation for your prior transgressions. To change your negative money perspective into a positive one, try reading books, blogs, viewing YouTube channels, and listening to personal finance podcasts!

Along with learning how to budget, save, and invest for the future of your finances, you will also learn how to improve your financial behavior.

11. Get inspiration from quotes about money thinking

Similar to affirmations, statements about money thinking can improve your outlook on life. Another benefit of reading quotes is the "coaching effect." They inspire and encourage you.

You can therefore greatly benefit from employing money mentality quotes to improve your financial mindset. To get you going, here are some of our favorite quotations:

"You are on the right track if broke people are making fun of your financial plan." - Unidentified

"Just take the first step; you don't need to see the entire staircase." - King, Martin Luther Jr.

"Even small changes to your everyday routine can have a significant impact on the results in your life." Darren Hardy "Extraordinary results do not always require extraordinary action." -Burkett Murray In chess, you should play as the player rather as the piece." Now is the moment to finally conquer the money game. - Tony Robbins.

Chapter 3

You can work two hours for yourself after eight hours of work for someone else

How to Get an Additional Two Hours Every Day

It's common to find oneself behind on your household to-do list and overworked at work. Sadly, most people find that there simply isn't enough time in the day to complete everything. To gain extra time in your day, you might start modifying your routine by carefully assessing your priorities and present schedule.

Eliminate or Combine Tasks That Consume the Most of Your Time

Think about changing the way you approach tasks or activities that occupy a significant portion of your day. Using your phone or the Internet, watching TV, checking email, and doing housework are a few examples.

Television and social media

The value that one derives from using Instagram, Netflix, or the Internet varies and is subjective. However, it's reasonable to believe that the majority of us occasionally indulge in vegging out. Try halving the amount of time you spend on the Internet and entertainment, or give up some activities completely (like TV) in an effort to prevent squandering time. You can set boundaries and break the habit with the aid of useful tools and site blockers! Bidding adieu to excessive social media or TV watching may even help you become healthier in addition to giving you extra hours in the day.

Tasks That Require Repeated Work

It's simple to become bogged down in work-related duties, particularly email. You should start to realize that you are wasting less time if you set up specific periods of the day to clean out your inbox and stop checking it on your phone every time you receive an email. An appropriate starting point? To give your colleagues time to act on your comments, clean up your inbox once in the morning and once at approximately 2:00 pm.

Tasks and run-arounds

It's difficult to keep a tidy and useful home or apartment. Certain tasks, like doing your laundry and dishwashing, are simply unavoidable. You can quickly start to find more time in your daily schedule by outsourcing domestic duties. Fortunately, Taskrabbit can assist you with everything else, Handy can help you find local housekeepers, and Rinse can take care of your laundry and dry cleaning. Your time is valuable, and if you're prepared to pay for assistance, services like these can help you get some (or a lot) of it back!

Make Better Use of Your Free Time Now

You'll start to see times when you're not making the most of your day when you start breaking it down. We advise you to consider how you may use your free time to do more significant tasks that you might not have time for at the moment. Among our recommendations are reading, studying, and creating. Rather than perusing your newsfeeds, establish a book (or Kindle book) with you at all times. Instead of using your phone to pass the time, attempt to fit in a little bit of reading every now and then.

Start listening to an audio book or podcast on your everyday commute. It's a fantastic way to pass the time while learning something new or engaging in entertainment without having to make any other schedule concessions.

Use time that would otherwise be wasted productively. Although it won't be simple to make significant adjustments to your lifestyle and schedule, we strongly advise looking into these options if you're serious about regaining an extra two hours each day.

The simplest way to get started is, by far, to outsource simpler chores like housecleaning and laundry. Removing these items from your list of things to accomplish will add up, and you'll start to notice the difference rather quickly.

You'll need to be proactive rather than reactive, be disciplined in maintaining consistency, and consider making more significant adjustments to your routine, such as getting up earlier in the morning, reducing or giving up non-essential kinds of entertainment, in order to maintain the change.

One of the main causes of creative project burnout is the intentional or unconscious decision to dedicate a whole day or week to a certain task. Let's face it: most of us will rarely have whole days to work on a project, and even then, we won't be able to finish it in that amount of time. We won't have that much creative energy left in us.

On the other hand, most audacious and imaginative undertakings are difficult to complete in 15- to 30-minute bursts. This kind of endeavor typically has an engagement barrier that means you need to allow yourself enough time to get set up and immerse yourself in the Flow. The natural reaction is to not start, as it is frustrating to not finish and difficult for most individuals to pick up where they left off.

It would be better to vacuum, check your email, or watch the latest meme on YouTube. (Since these things are important.) Finally, when you do decide to chunk your work into smaller portions, it can be very difficult to choose how much to do so.

Introducing the Two-Hour Rule

Divide up your creative work into blocks of two hours. You can accomplish a lot in two hours, but it's not so long that it becomes tedious.

The following are some explanations for why the Two-Hour Rule is effective

It monitors our circadian cycles and creative energies in real life. While everyone's cycles are a little bit different, most people experience a creative or circadian cycle around every two hours.

In optimal conditions, peak-performing creatives can often keep their energy for only four to six hours; most of us are unable to focus at that level for longer than two hours, and our productivity starts to drop after that.

Most people can leave a room for up to two hours without anything catching fire. Many creative people hold the unhelpful assumption that they must always be aware of what's going on. Although they don't explicitly tell themselves that, their behavior suggests otherwise. If you find it difficult to dedicate two hours of your day to anything, there may be more serious problems underlying your creative work, such as codependency, overcommitment, inadequate expectation management, etc. You can find it difficult to hold onto your job and take a break throughout the workday if you are employed by a business with weak communication procedures and even worse expectations.

Similar to this, you can find it more difficult to firewall your time if your job involves a lot of reactive work, such as customer service; in that situation, being reactively effective is productive.

Finding two hours each day to repurpose for the things that really matter is surprisingly easy. Cut one or two TV programs. Rise a little bit sooner. Take your children to bed earlier. You'll figure it out if it's important to you.

We all know how much we can accomplish in two hours, most of us. Likewise "how many words can you write in two hours?" In much amount of words can you write in a day? You get the idea. Just replace "write" with your creative endeavor. It facilitates our ability to think in natural time blocks as opposed to arbitrary hours. Instead of batching chores and household work, spread them out over the week in the evenings when you're tired and can't do anything creative anyhow; then use the afternoons you would have been doing chores to work on your project. Though minor, this one is nonetheless significant.

The concept of hours is a relatively new approach to divide up human experience; in contrast, the ability to recognize time blocks is one of the many characteristics that comprise self-awareness. Our unconscious experience is given an unconscious unit by our psychochemical cycles. More than that, though, is that it makes planning easier on both a daily and project level. Saying "that'll take me four creative blocks" is more manageable than "that'll take me eight hours" if you understand it, as you'll know how much work you can accomplish in a creative block, which is two hours. The next time you're considering beginning a project or figuring out how to divide it up, apply the Two-Hour Rule to make it easier.

A little secret: you may need to allow yourself two hours of leisure while also telling yourself that you just need to spend ten minutes on any necessary tasks. If you set restrictions for yourself on both ends, you'll probably create for two hours.

Anthony L. Thomas and Bartholomew O. Utazi

Chapter 4

Expert Budgeting

Expert Budgeting Techniques

A sound financial strategy is essential for controlling expenses. A well-planned personal budget will track savings progress, anticipate unforeseen costs like birthdays, and help uncover unhealthy spending patterns. If adhered to over an extended period, it will enhance fiscal self-control and offer comfort. Research indicates that writing down our goals increases our chances of success, whether they are financial or not. So how precisely can you create a household budget that makes the most financial sense? And how do you ensure that, in the face of temptation, you stay true to it?

Examine your expenditures

Even if we all have a general concept of our monthly expenses, forensic examination of bank statements frequently reveals a totally different picture. Paul Merriman, CEO of Ask Paul and Pax Financial, says, "Budgeting starts with acknowledgement and awareness, so we always advise our clients to analyze their bank statements over a six-month time frame, not including the Christmas period." "You may believe you're spending a certain amount, say, on coffee, but upon closer inspection of your statement, you may find that you're actually spending much less or much more."

Be sincere with yourself

Examining bank statements may be a dismal experience, particularly when calculating the monthly expenses associated with vices like drinking, smoking, and gambling.

According to John Lowe of Money Doctors, it might be a moment of realization, but it's crucial to be truthful. "At the end of the day, nobody is looking at these figures except yourself, so there's no point in fooling yourself."

Reduce wasteful spending

According to Mr. Merriman, the next stage is to identify the monthly costs that can be cut or eliminated. "Ask yourself if this is adding any value. Get rid of anything that doesn't add value. Is it possible to obtain it for a more affordable price if it offers value? It's critical to adopt a long-term perspective while examining your outgoings, he adds.

Control recurrent subscriptions

Your financial accounts will probably include recurring subscriptions that cost less than $6 a month once you go through them all. While these subscriptions are meant to simplify life, they are also purposefully hard to cancel. Mr. Merriman advises, "If you're not using it, cancel it—even if it bothers you to do so." He notes that some of his customers don't even realize they have monthly subscriptions.

Decide on a money ratio

Maintaining a personal finance ratio will assist you in staying on course each month. The 50/30/20 Rule, as suggested by Lorraine Donegan of Donegan Financial Services, states that you should set aside 50% for necessities (such as a mortgage, bills, and food); 30% for wants (such as clothes shopping, eating out, and vacations); and 20% for savings, including pension. After paying for his needs, Mr. Merriman would rather divide his remaining funds into three equal parts. "A third is allocated to emergency funds, a third is used for living expenses, and the other third is invested in little amounts that are progressively increased over time. It requires time and patience to break the cycle of your money working for you instead of you working for it.

Establish objectives (and treat yourself along the way)

Financial discipline can be developed through budgeting, but having a goal in mind will make it much simpler to maintain motivation and withstand spending temptations. Mr. Merriman asserts that "it's very difficult to keep yourself on a financial pathway when you don't set goals." "You must be making progress toward something, whether it's six months away or 10 years away." He goes on, "It's important to reward yourself once you reach a savings target." "Treat yourself to a purse, a vacation, or whatever else you want, and then go again. You cannot move toward a goal psychologically without any intermediate steps.

Check out online banking

According to Ms. Donegan, digital banks like Revolut and N26 make budget tracking simpler. "These days, people want more visually appealing budget plans, and I just don't have the time to visit the bank, much less download statements and go through transactions," the woman claims. "Payments made using digital banking apps are automatically categorized, allowing you to view logos for restaurants, Starbucks, and other businesses next to your historical spending patterns. It makes saving money for immediate needs and exercising financial restraint simpler.

Make family financial planning a priority

When everyone is on board, budgets function best. Make it honest and "You should be aware of what is happening to your money if your name appears on a document."

In line with Ms. Donegan, household budgets can also aid in teaching kids about financial literacy. "Hopefully, if you teach them to physically save money at a young age, it will stick with them as a habit later in life."

Play around with various methods and applications

If all of this seems like too much work, consider downloading a spreadsheet or streamlined app that tracks your spending by category and notifies you when you go over your budget. To obtain a budget spreadsheet, send an email to info@moneydoctors.ie. Money Doctors offers a self-calculating spreadsheet at no cost.

Try the envelope approach

If you've already given up on household budgeting or if you're searching for anything even simpler to adhere to. You deposit money into several envelopes at the beginning of each month according to budget categories (e.g., "dining out and takeaways," "coffees," "beauty and clothes shopping"), and you only spend the amount that is available in the envelopes. The hands-on approach reduces overspending in part because every category is meticulously budgeted and in part because giving up cash is more emotionally taxing.

Chapter 5

Financial Leverage

What Does Financial Leverage Mean?

Leveraging financial resources by taking out a loan in order to invest in assets is a calculated risk. The intention is for the return on those assets to outweigh the interest paid on the loans used to purchase them. Financial leverage aims to boost investor profitability without requiring the use of extra personal funds. When a company uses borrowed capital to fund investments to increase its asset base and produce returns on risk capital, it is said to be using financial leverage. Leverage is an investment technique that increases an investment's potential return by employing borrowed money, or more specifically, the employment of different financial instruments or borrowed capital. A company's debt-to-asset ratio can also be referred to as **leverage**.

Comprehending Financial Leverage

Using debt or borrowed funds to fund an investment or activity is known as leverage. It is frequently employed to increase the equity basis of an entity. Leverage is a concept that businesses and investors use.

Leverage is a tool used by investors to dramatically raise the possible returns on their investments. They use a variety of tools, such as margin accounts, futures, and options, to increase the leverage on their assets. Businesses can finance their assets by using leverage.

Put another way, firms can utilize debt financing to invest in business operations in an effort to maximize shareholder value, as an alternative to selling shares to obtain capital.

There are many ways for investors to obtain leverage indirectly if they feel uncomfortable employing it directly. Without raising their outlay, they can invest in businesses that fund or expand operations using leverage in the regular course of business.

The purpose and outcome of financial leverage are to increase a project's possible returns. Leverage will also increase the possible downside risk in the event that the investment is a failure. If a business, asset, or investment is described as "highly leveraged," it indicates that it has more debt than equity.

One possible contributing factor to the global financial crisis of 2008 was leverage. Some think that rather than accepting meager returns, borrowers and investment firms became avaricious and took on leveraged positions, and when their leveraged bets underperformed, they put themselves up to significant market consequences.

How to Calculate Your Leverage Amount

To determine how much debt a business is leveraging in an effort to maximize profits, a variety of leverage financial ratios are available. The list below includes some typical leverage ratios.

Ratio of total debt to total assets

By determining the percentage of its assets that were acquired through loans, a business can assess how leveraged it is. To calculate the equity-to-assets ratio, a business might deduct the total debt-to-total-assets ratio from 1.

A corporation that has a high debt-to-assets ratio has likely financed its assets mostly through leverage.

Total Debt ÷ Total Assets is the total debt-to-assets ratio. Remember that all debt, including both short- and long-term debt vehicles, is used to compute the ratio.

Ratio of Debt to Equity (D/E)

Rather than focusing on the company's assets, leverage can be measured by closely examining the financing of its assets. A comparison between the amount borrowed by the

company and the amount raised from shareholders or private investors is made using the debt-to-equity (D/E) ratio.

Total Debt ÷ Total Equity is the debt-to-equity ratio.

A corporation has more debt than equity if its debt-to-equity ratio is greater than one. This does not, however, imply that a business is overly leveraged. Every business and sector usually functions differently, which could mean a different ratio.

For instance, fledgling technology businesses frequently have to rely on private investors in order to obtain funding. As a result, a debt-to-equity ratio of 0.5 would still be regarded as excessive in this sector.

Ratio of Debt to EBITDA

A business can also evaluate its debt in relation to its revenue for a specific time frame. The ability to control debt in relation to operating income will be important to the organization. For this reason, EBITDA is frequently used rather than net income.

A business that has a large debt-to-EBITDA ratio is heavily indebted relative to its earnings. More leverage indicates a higher debt-to-EBITDA ratio for the organization.

Total Debt ÷ Earnings Before Interest, Taxes, Depreciation, and Amortization equals debt-to-EBITDA.

Multiplier for Equity

In the equity multiplier, debt is not taken into account explicitly. However, it is included by default because total debt is directly correlated with both total assets and total equity. The equity multiplier looks at how assets have been financed in an effort to determine a company's ownership weight. A business that has a low equity multiplier is not excessively leveraged because a significant portion of its assets have been financed with equity.

The multiplier for equity is Total Assets ÷ Total Equity.

The equity multiplier is a tool used in DuPont analysis to quantify financial leverage. The equity multiplier can be computed by dividing the total assets of a company by the entire equity. To calculate return on equity, multiply total financial leverage by total asset turnover plus profit margin.

For instance, the equity multiplier is 2.0 ($500 million ÷ $250 million) if a publicly traded corporation has $500 million in total assets and $250 million in shareholder equity.

This demonstrates that equity has financed half of the company's total assets. Larger equity multipliers, therefore, imply higher levels of financial leverage.

Leverage Level in Finance (DFL)

The degree of financial leverage is used in fundamental analysis (DFL). The DFL is computed by dividing the percentage change in a company's profits before interest and taxes (EBIT) during a given period by the percentage change in its earnings per share (EPS).

Percentage Change in Earnings Per Share ÷ Percentage Change in EBIT = Degree of Financial Leverage

Determining how responsive an organization's earnings per share (EPS) is to variations in operational income is the aim of DFL.

A corporation with a high DFL is probably going to have more fluctuating earnings; a greater ratio will suggest a higher level of leverage.

The ratio of consumer leverage

Firms that employ leverage in their operations applies the calculations mentioned above. Households, however, can also employ leverage. Households can also employ leverage by taking out debt and using their own income to pay interest. The calculation of consumer leverage involves dividing the debt of a household by its disposable income. households with greater computed consumer leverage are highly leveraged because they have greater debt-to-income ratios.

Total household debt divided by disposable income is consumer leverage. If a consumer's consumer leverage rises too high, they may eventually have trouble getting loans. Lenders, for instance, frequently impose debt-to-income ceilings on households applying for mortgage loans.

Financial ratios are most valuable when compared to competitors or over an extended period of time. When comparing the leverage ratios of different organizations, keep in mind that different financing arrangements may be appropriate for different industries.

Benefits and Drawbacks of Financial Leverage

Benefits

Leverage is typically used by traders and investors to increase profits. When additional upfront funds are added to your initial investment, winners can become much more profitable. Leverage also gives you access to more expensive investment possibilities that a modest quantity of upfront capital would not normally grant.

When large amounts of capital are required in short-term, low-risk scenarios, leverage can be employed. For instance, a growing business may require funding in the near term for acquisitions or buyouts, which could present a significant mid-to-long-term growth opportunity. Rather than taking on more debt to fund reckless ventures, astute businesses use leverage to seize opportunities when they present themselves, with the goal of rapidly unloading their leveraged position.

Drawbacks

Losing investments increase in proportion to winning ones. Leverage increases the downside risk significantly and can lead to losses larger than the initial capital commitment in certain cases.

In addition, commissions, fees, and margin rates are frequently assessed by brokers and contract traders. This implies that additional fees will still apply even if your trade ends in a loss.

Complexity is another possible drawback of leverage. When taking a leveraged position, investors need to understand their financial situation and the dangers involved. If a trader's account does not have enough equity as required by their broker, they may need to pay closer attention to their portfolio and contribute more money.

Leverage Pros

Leverage increases the possibility of large earnings by amplifying profitable investments.

lowers entry barriers by giving investors access to more lucrative trading opportunities.

A calculated approach for businesses to satisfy their short-term funding requirements for buyouts or acquisitions.

Cons

Enhances investment losses by generating the possibility of significant losses. More costly compared to alternative trading methods results in higher costs, contract premiums, and margin rates, irrespective of the trade's success, and is more intricate since, depending on the needs of the portfolio, trading may demand more time and money.

Financial Margin versus Leverage

Margin is a unique kind of leverage that allows one to raise their buying power in the financial markets by pledging their current cash or securities position as collateral.

With margin, you can borrow money at a fixed interest rate from a broker to buy equities, options, or futures contracts with the hope of making significantly large profits.

Leverage can be created through margin, which increases your purchasing power by the entire balance in your margin account. For example, you would have a 1:10 margin or 10x leverage if you needed $1,000 in collateral to buy $10,000 worth of assets.

Financial Leverage Examples

A business was established with a $5 million investment from investors; the $5 million represents the company's equity. If the corporation borrows $20 million through debt financing, it will have an additional $25 million to invest in operations and more chances to boost shareholder value.

For instance, a car manufacturer could take out a loan to construct a new plant. The new facility would enable the corporation to produce more cars and increase revenue. The business now has five times the capital available for use toward its expansion, as opposed to being restricted to the $5 million from investors. In the financial markets, positions with this kind of leverage are common. For instance, in March 2022, Apple (AAPL) released $4.7 billion in Green Bonds for the third time.

Apple might increase its use of debt financing to grow its low-carbon production and generate chances for recycling while using carbon-free aluminum. This kind of approach is effective when revenue is higher than bond costs.

Chapter 6

Make Financial Decisions Automatically

How much time do you spend each month paying payments, monitoring your balances, and transferring money around? Is it several hours, perhaps a half-day? If you find yourself devoting nearly all of your time to these chores, it's probably more than you ought to. You may automate your finances to require almost little time commitment each month with the help of contemporary tools and apps. The numerous transfers, payments, and transactions involved in handling household finances can be extremely time- and energy-consuming. You can recover that time and energy, as well as the assurance that your finances are steady, safe, and rapidly approaching your future, by putting the entire system on autopilot.

Streamline Your Budget and Bills

Monthly financial transactions for a regular home can total hundreds, ranging from housing and utilities to daily spending. Some things, like a trip to the grocery store, are inevitable. Without the right procedures in place, some, like the phone bill, can easily fall between the cracks and lead to more problems. And keeping track of and managing these transactions is essential for preserving financial well-being in every situation.

1. **Bill payment online**

You're probably not making the most of the modern miracle of automatic bill pay if you still have to sit down every month to pay the bills. There are two main methods that automatic bill payment can occur:

The "push" method entails providing your bank with the biller's details so that it can transmit (or push) automatic payments on your behalf.

The "pull" method, in which the biller obtains your bank account or credit card details and proceeds to deduct the amount owed from your accounts.

When possible, push-style bill pay is preferred since it gives you more security and control over the amount and timing of the withdrawals of your funds. Pull-style ePay, however, can be your sole choice for expenses that aren't usually a set amount, including credit card payments and utilities. With these two techniques, almost any bill, payment, or expense can now be automated.

But be careful not to allow the convenience of eBill pay fool you into forgetting about your payments completely. It is a good idea to monitor your expenditures and know how much you are spending on each item even if you are not required to perform the tedious task of paying them by hand.

2. Track Your Budget with Apps

Divergent views exist on conventional budgeting. According to some experts, in order to preserve healthy spending habits, households should keep a tight eye on each and every expense and category. Some people support a less rigorous method of creating a budget. But almost everyone concurs that it's a good idea for everyone to periodically assess their expenditures and make necessary adjustments to their habits.

One of the most important things you can do to improve your financial situation is to be aware of where your money is going and how much you frequently spend. Still, very few individuals actually do it. The fact that it's a chore that requires a lot of time and is typically not enjoyable is one of the primary causes. The workload associated with budget tracking is significantly reduced when it is automated, which makes it much simpler to maintain the habit.

This procedure is made extremely simple by a number of financial programs, such as Mint and YNAB, which track and categorize your monthly expenses, saves, and more automatically. Your only remaining task is to stop by and take a few minutes each month to review the outcomes!

3. Establish Budgetary Boundaries

As many of us do, if you struggle with impulsive buys and overspending, technology might be able to help. Certain debit and credit cards let you establish a spending cap on your account. A spending limit is a barrier that serves as a reminder when you reach a spending threshold you don't want to go over, distinct from your credit limit on that account.

These caps serve as a contemporary alternative to the more conventional analog envelope system, which allows you to set spending caps in several categories by separating your cash into designated envelopes. For many years, the envelope method has been a well-liked tactic that has significantly improved people's spending patterns. These advantages are carried over into the age of digital transfers and electronic payments with automated spending limitations.

4. Reduce Debt While You're Sleeping

You probably have the most of this if you followed the instructions to automate your bill payment. Automatic payments can significantly impact individuals striving to eliminate their debt. Numerous separate loans, liens, and credit lines, each with its own terms and monthly payment, may make up a household's total debt. Manually making these payments is quite time-consuming and comes with a risk of fines, interest, and credit damage if even one payment gets lost.

You don't need to stop there; setting up auto-pay to pay the minimal amounts on all of your obligations is a huge step toward financial security.

If your current financial aim is to pay off debt rapidly, you might want to set up an auto-payment that is higher than the minimum. Ideally, just attempt this on a single loan at a time, and observe as it dissolves away, one by one.

Automate Your Savings and Banking

On paper, saving money could sound tedious. That is, unless the document was a balance sheet that demonstrated the cumulative impact of a consistent saving practice on your life. Nevertheless, over time, the tangible benefits of fervently conserving money might be enormous. Even better, practically everything can be done automatically. Savings can be made easier and more efficient by automating them, which also removes stress and work from the process. Here's how you can benefit from it.

5. Utilize Auto-Transfers to Save

One financial tip that is so often shared that it has become cliché is to "pay yourself first." That is to say, set aside a portion of your money for your goals and savings before you pay for anything else.

Certain things are cliched for a purpose. Making savings a priority helps you balance your daily life with your long-term objectives.

Paying yourself first on a regular basis is made simple with auto-transfers; you don't even have to think about it. While you carry on with your life, automatic transfers—like a monthly deposit from a checking to a savings account—allow you to progressively accumulate wealth in the background. This is an option that most online bank accounts provide. Check to see if you may immediately begin auto-saving after logging in! Of course, on top of this foundation, you can always save a little extra each month. By automating it, all it does is add a monthly minimum accomplishment to your wealth.

6. Use Overdraft Protection to Avoid Fees

One of the more neglected secrets to wealth-building is the necessity of avoiding fees and other avoidable charges. Even though an occasional late fee or additional cost might seem like a small annoyance, over time they can significantly reduce your ability to accumulate wealth. Specifically, overdraft fees can be a sneaky (and needless) expense. Overdraft fees cost Americans billions of dollars annually. But with a little mechanization, it is largely preventable for the majority.

See whether overdraft protection is a service your bank provides. Though there are other methods as well, one of the safest is just bringing in the necessary funds from a linked account. For example, you can instruct your bank to automatically take money out of your savings account to meet the overdraft amount and save you a high overdraft fee if you overdraw your checking account.

This approach will only be effective if you have the funds available to make the purchase, which is not always the case. Therefore, this kind of overdraft protection isn't a foolproof way to prevent money shortages. However, overdraft protection is an obvious win for automation in terms of preventing needless expenses brought on by just losing track.

7. Configure Alerts and Unwind

Like with account spending limitations, you may utilize automated alerts to simplify and stabilize your financial life by avoiding needless worry and hassle. With the knowledge that you are keeping an eye on your finances without physically being there all the time, you can rest easy knowing that you are receiving alerts for unexpected expenses, foreign charges, and overspending in a certain category.

Alerts from credit monitoring services can also tell you about possible identity and data theft. You can customize these alerts to match your interests and concerns in a number of ways. The greatest places to start would be any software you use for budgeting and financial tracking, as well as your bank or credit card company.

Automate Your Financial and Investing Objectives

Similar to increasing your cash reserves, investing for the future frequently gains from a reduction in daily interpersonal interaction. You may set your investment account for significantly higher development by letting the robots handle the driving and depending less on good investing practices.

8. Autonomously Cruise to Retirement

Employer-sponsored retirement plans, such as 401(k)s and pensions, have a significant benefit that is hardly discussed enough. No, it's not the confusing power of compound interest or the significant tax benefits. Not even employer matching is involved. Naturally, these are all wonderful advantages and important factors in the high value of these accounts. However, you were probably already aware of all those details. The fact that these accounts are automated subtly adds far more value to them than anything else.

Employer-sponsored plans were designed to facilitate passive capital accumulation. Most people find it difficult to deliberately and reliably save money for retirement without the help of instruments like these. Making the most of these accounts, if available, is one of the best things you can do for your financial future. By setting up an IRA with monthly automated payments, anyone can give themselves the same opportunity even if they are not eligible for workplace matching schemes.

9. Simmer the Frog to Reach Your Money Objectives

A technique known as "boiling the frog" involves starting something out slowly and painlessly and then gradually increasing your approach over time. Though there are many applications for this mode of thinking, personal finance and the "boil the frog" approach mesh well together.

For example, boiling the frog could mean contributing a small amount each month at first, then gradually increasing it once or twice a year in order to save money. Alternatively, let's say you want to start saving for retirement by contributing 6% of your salary to a 401(k).

After that, you may raise it to 6.5% or 7% annually. Without having an adverse effect on your lifestyle, you may save 10% or more of your monthly income for retirement by taking one tiny, almost perceptible step at a time.

You can choose to automatically take advantage of this option in many 401(k)-like plans and some banks. Consider this as a kind of meta-step to some of the other automation models we have previously examined: Not only can you automate your retirement or savings contributions, but you can also automate the process of progressively raising them.

10. Use Robots to Boost Your Regular Investing Game

Historically, ordinary people have relied heavily on financial experts like brokers and accountants to help them choose and manage their investments. For regular investors these days, it is becoming less and less the case. The phrase "robo-advisors" refers to the array of financial planning and investing tools that families can now access through Wealthfront and Betterment. These applications can assist with investing selection based on your time horizon and risk tolerance. They can also assist with portfolio rebalancing and other strategic actions like dollar-cost averaging.

At a fraction of the cost of a traditional advisor, they can fulfill the majority of your requests, and best of all, they can handle it all automatically in the background. All you need to do is keep adding funds, and the robots will take care of the rest.

11. Set Up Auto-Distributions

You can automate your money's entry into your investments as well as its exit back to you. Automation can assist when you're ready to start taking withdrawals from your investments, whether you're in traditional retirement, at a point in your FIRE path, or at any other moment.

At a time when stability is most welcome, regular, automated distributions from an investment account or retirement plan offer certainty to life.

Even if you pay your own expenses, knowing exactly how much money you make each month will help you stick to a budget and limit your spending. Knowing precisely how quickly you're depleting your nest egg to prevent it from running out too soon also gives you piece of mind. Not just at the start of your financial journey, but at every turn, automation can be a blessing.

Things Not to Automate

It is important to remember that not every aspect of your financial life should be automated, even though practically every inch of it can be. Most of the time, automation can help you manage your finances more emotionally and save a ton of time, as demonstrated by the examples we've looked at here. And this works perfectly for things like paying bills, transferring money, and contributing to your objectives.

However, there are a few areas where a human touch will still have a significant positive impact on your finances. You will still want to be involved in the "personal" aspect of your finances even when computers and robots manage the day-to-day "finance" aspect. You should really, truly pay attention to things like creating and modifying your financial goals, choosing the route you want to follow to get there, and determining the overall kind of financial life you want to have. Additionally, you'll free up your time and energy to concentrate on these more crucial matters by letting automation take care of all the tedious tasks!

The Autonomous Road to Wealth: Put It and Forget It

Nowadays, you may discover features, tools, and apps to automate nearly all of the tiresome or difficult tasks related to personal finance. These resources can help you develop better financial habits and pave the way for your future while also saving you a great deal of time and effort.

The custom of sitting down at the kitchen table to manage household finances has become all but obsolete due to the conveniences of the information age. Certain things are always going to require a little more hands-on care than others, such as reaching financial objectives. You'll have all the time you need for that, though, since everything else will be automated and out of the way.

Chapter 7

Net Worth Factor

Your Net Worth: What Is It?

Your net worth is the sum of all of your assets minus all of your liabilities. It is the entire worth of everything you own, such as your home, vehicles, investments, and cash, less everything you owe on debt (such as credit card debt, school loans, and the remaining balance on your mortgage). With the help of our Net Worth Calculator, we have made it simpler for you to determine that amount. Your net worth can be calculated in five minutes by simply responding to a few short questions—less time than it takes to have your morning coffee!

Calculating Net Worth: What Constitutes Assets and Liabilities?

Your capacity to calculate net worth is dependent on your ability to define exactly what is an asset and what is a liability. So, before you begin calculating, let's make it obvious what belongs in each column:

Assets

Assets come in two varieties: liquid and illiquid. A liquid asset is essentially easily accessible cash, such as funds in a money market account. Conversely, an illiquid asset cannot be rapidly turned into cash. That would be anything you would need to sell in order to get money, such a car or a plot of land. Your net worth calculation takes into account both kinds of assets, which may include:

Cash: checking and savings accounts 401(k), 403(b), and IRA retirement accounts, among other investment vehicles.

Real estate: your home's current worth and any rental properties you own automobiles, trucks, and boats.

Items in your home collection: artwork, jewelry, and so forth.

Liabilities

The not so enjoyable part is about to begin: totaling up all of your liabilities. All of your outstanding debts and payments are considered liabilities. It's essentially the things you owe other people. Items like as: credit histories, student loans, mortgages, auto loans, medical expenses, etc.

Naturally, it is ideal if all of your obligations are zero, meaning you have no debts. If that isn't the case (yet), list all of your bills and using the debt snowball method to pay them off as soon as you can. Your net worth will increase as your liabilities decrease!

How Your Net Worth Is Determined

Your net worth can be determined in three simple steps.

First, total up your Assets (what you own).

Once more, everything that you own that is worth money is considered an asset; this includes everything from your 401(k) account and savings to the vehicle parked in your driveway. Therefore, compile a list of your assets to get things started. Assume for the moment that you own these:

a $210,000 home and a $60,000 401(k)

vehicle with a $15,000 price tag

$7,000 in the savings account.

Verifying the $2,000 sum in my account, your entire assets come to $294,000 when you add everything together.

Step 2: Total Your Debts (Amounts Due)

Regretfully, it's possible that you have some outstanding debt. Take out a mortgage (a 15-year fixed-rate loan is OK) and any outstanding medical expenses you may have. You might have also made some "stupid" financial decisions over the years, accruing credit card debt and auto loans (haven't we all?). What you owe is as follows:

debt from credit cards totaling $12,000,

$35,000 in outstanding student loan debt,

$175,000 remains on the mortgage.

$10,000 for a car loan

$1,000 in medical expenses.

The total of your liabilities is $233,000.

Step Three: Deduct Your Liabilities From Your Assets

All that's left to do is use this formula to subtract: Total Liabilities minus Total Assets = Net Worth. Thus, $61,000 is your total net worth: $193,000 in liabilities minus $294,000 in assets equals $61,000 in net worth.

The Reasons for Knowing Your Net Worth

Determining your financial situation is the first step towards determining your net worth. And while that's a good place to start, you must go farther! Finding out your net worth is meant to serve as a starting point for
achieving your financial objectives.

This is the method.

1. Your net worth indicates your position

Do you have enough money saved for retirement? Do you have enough cash in your savings to deal with an unforeseen expense? Which debts do you need to pay off first? Your net worth will assist you in responding to these queries. It helps you see things clearly in your current circumstances.

It's acceptable if you don't like where you are. The game is still ongoing! You still have time to make up lost ground in your money growth. Until you give up, you are never truly out of the game. Don't give up; keep going. Find methods to go forward, maintain your attention on the next objective in front of you, and remain focused.

2. Your net worth indicates what requires adjustment

Your debts should ideally equal a big, fat zero. However, determining your net worth compels you to assess your options if you do have debt. Unidentified problems are impossible to solve. Apply the debt snowball strategy to bid debt a fond farewell. Sort your debts by amount, starting with the smallest, and pay them off as soon as you can. Not only will paying off debt increase your income, but it will also increase your net worth! Perhaps you should tow the truck away in the driveway. You may have to sell so much that the children believe you're the next big thing. Make every effort to eliminate debt from your life!

You're doing fantastically if the only debt you still have is your mortgage. However, keep your foot on the gas at this point. Could you accelerate the payoff of your house even further by making a few more mortgage payments annually? With no debt and no more property payments, just think of how much money you could invest for the future!

3. Your Net Worth Indicates How Much Work Remains

We argue that accumulating wealth is more akin to a marathon than a sprint, and if that's the case, you ought to be aware of the destination! If your net worth indicates where you stand in the race, then the amount you must save for retirement indicates how far you still have to go.

The good news is that you can calculate exactly how much money you need to retire and how much you need to invest each month to get there using our free tool.

You can even experiment with different amounts of savings and spending to see what happens. Everyone will have a different number, but in order to avoid running in circles, it's critical to have a target in sight!

Anomalies Regarding Net Worth

Let's discuss what your net worth isn't now that you know what it is. To begin with, your possessions do not make up your entire net worth. Even if you have a million dollars in investments and cash, if another million dollars are being used for credit card debt, student loans, and mortgages, you are not wealthy—you are bankrupt!

Furthermore, your salary does not equal your net worth! A person's high salary may not always translate into a high net worth. There's a misconception in our society that building wealth requires having a high salary. As genuine as a three-dollar bill is that delusion. Even while a six-figure salary could be beneficial, poor financial management won't make you wealthy. The greatest and most thorough research study of millionaires in history was concluded by Ramsey Solutions.

To find out what a true millionaire looks like, they spoke with over 10,000 millionaires, or people whose net worth is at least $1 million. You might be surprised by what we found.

Here's a tip: Everyone has the potential to become a millionaire over time, regardless of their salary, occupation, or educational background. Dave tells the tales of actual people in his best-selling book Baby Steps Millionaires who, despite having average wages, went on to become millionaires as a result of their same behaviors and routines that can make you a millionaire too!

Chapter 8

Avoiding needless taxes

The history of taxes extends back to the time of the ancient civilizations. Around 2500 BCE, the earliest known tax systems developed in Mesopotamia, where farmers gave rulers a share of their harvest. Taxation was also used by Rome and Ancient Egypt to finance public works projects. Feudal lords imposed taxes on their subjects in the Middle Ages. The 19th century saw the establishment of modern income taxes, most notably in Britain in 1799. Income tax was first imposed in the US during the Civil War, and the 16th Amendment made it a permanent institution in 1913.

Taxes are a vital source of finance for governments across the globe today. We all have to deal with the inevitable evil of paying taxes, but thankfully, there are ways to lessen the annual tax load you have to bear. There are completely legal ways to lower your tax liability without engaging in dubious business dealings or elaborate plans that could put you in legal hot water. This post will examine and offer advice on how to legally avoid paying taxes. We will examine investments, tax credits, and deductions that may help you keep more of your money in your pocket and reduce your taxable income.

Tax Evasion vs. Tax Avoidance

Regarding tax avoidance vs tax evasion, there are several common misconceptions. Individuals frequently combine the two when, in fact, they are entirely different concepts.

Avoidance of taxes

Taking advantage of any tax credits, deductions, or other tax-reducing incentives made available by a tax system constitutes tax avoidance, which is entirely lawful. Tax evasion and tax avoidance examples are sometimes confused because many taxpayers are ignorant of the easy ways to legitimately avoid paying taxes. Cyprus's non-resident taxation scheme is among the greatest schemes for tax evasion. This program permits any foreign national who was not a resident prior to the start of their job to receive a 20 percent exemption from gross taxable income from employment performed in Cyprus, up to a maximum of €8,550 ($9,117).

Evading taxes

However, tax evasion is the unlawful practice of purposefully concealing income or making up financial information to avoid or underpay taxes. It's basically avoiding paying taxes that you owe by lowering your responsibility, as opposed to finding a way to legally avoid paying them. While concealing or falsifying income is the main component of tax evasion, there are several ways in which it can be committed.

Here are a few instances of tax avoidance:

Not disclosing earnings: Underreporting income on tax returns from a job, including tips or salary, failing to record revenue from investments, including real estate or businesses, or failing to report any other sources of income are examples of failing to report income.

Making fictitious claims for business expenditures, exaggerating the value of charity contributions, or deducting items from personal expenses are examples of making fictitious claims for deductions.

Transferring taxable assets overseas: To conceal and render taxable assets untraceable to tax authorities, taxable assets are transferred to an offshore bank account.

Shell businesses: By setting up a dummy firm, typically overseas or in a tax haven, one might use shell companies to channel revenue or profits in a way that distorts real earnings.

Using corporate assets for personal use: The use of a company's tangible assets, such as real estate, vehicles, and equipment, as well as its intangible assets, such as business databases and intellectual property, for purposes other than work is known as "using corporate assets for personal use."

How Independent Contractors Can Lawfully Avoid or Lower Taxes

Regarding federal income taxes, there are benefits to operating as a freelancer as opposed to an employee. First of all, you have greater influence over the taxes you pay as opposed to income tax, which is routinely withheld by your employer from your paycheck. Particularly well with expenses is freelance job. Unlike spending on income from freelancing, the description of how to avoid tax on salary through expenses would be more involved. You have the option to deduct expenses from your tax bill prior to payment, as opposed to requesting a refund for them.

Self-employed people and remote freelancers are also allowed to benefit from foreign tax incentives, such as Portugal's NHR tax scheme (non-habitual resident), which lowers the tax rates on income produced in Portugal. For instance, if you work as a freelancer in Portugal and earn €55,000 ($58,600) but are not a resident, you will pay a flat tax rate of 20 percent instead of the 43.5 percent national rate for residents. More information about this program is available.

Tax deduction for self-employment

Taking full advantage of a self-employment tax deduction scheme is one of the easiest ways to reduce your tax liability or even pay nothing at all. If your self-employed income meets certain permissible expenses, you can deduct a portion of it from your taxable profit in the United States.

Income Tax on Employment

For the self-employment tax deduction to be applicable, you have to be:

An individual business owner

An associate within a collaboration

An individual with limited liability company (LLC)

Someone who submits their tax return together with a Schedule C or Schedule C-EZ (Form 1040). You can declare your self-employed income in the "Other Taxes" section of Form 1040 and claim the self-employment tax deduction on your Schedule SE (Form 1040) if any of the aforementioned conditions are met. The IRS will distinguish between the federal income tax and the self-employed tax in this manner.

Let's take the scenario where you are a lone entrepreneur and your net revenue from freelancing is $80,000. You would owe the IRS $6,120 in self-employment taxes if the current tax rate of 15.3 percent, which is applied to 50% of your income, were to be followed. Your taxable income would be $73,880, though, as you are permitted to subtract that amount from your self-employed income when filing taxes. Consequently, you would save $936.

Every tax year, this plan can save you a substantial sum of money on your taxes. If you believe you may be eligible for this deduction, find out if you qualify by speaking with a tax expert.

Subtract for operating costs

As a freelancer, you can deduct a range of business expenditures from your taxable income within a given calendar year. Even if you work from home, you can deduct expenses for marketing, office supplies, and travel. It is imperative that you maintain documentation of all your yearly deductions for company expenses and ensure that you are aware of the goods that qualify for tax exemptions.

Additionally, you must make sure that you only deduct business-related expenses in accordance with tax rules. If not, you risk facing severe fines from the Internal Revenue Service or another federal tax authority.

The normal mileage deduction can be utilized as an additional method of deducting business expenses. You can deduct a specific amount using this strategy for each mile you drive on business travel. Given that it remains an expense for any business owner, the makes sense in the long run.

This may not always be appropriate when traveling to and from work, but it can be utilized when attending meetings.

For small business owners, this is especially important because time spent traveling may result in lower revenue.

Most people overlook the fact that business travel and educational costs are also deductible. Certain nations allow you to include information about your primary source of income or side business in your personal tax return. Just remember to follow your country's tax regulations and make sure all of your filings utilize the correct tax code. If not, you risk having to refund a hefty amount in federal income taxes, swiftly turning your tax benefit into a nightmare. Regardless of the approach you take to figure out your business expenses, be sure to maintain detailed records of everything you spend. This will assist you in averting future issues and facilitate the presentation of proof of expenditure upon request.

Make a retirement plan contribution

There are various ways in which a freelancer might make contributions to a retirement plan. One of the simplest legal methods to prevent paying excessive or insufficient taxes is to do this. If you're an American citizen, there are two typical methods to accomplish this. These are the following:

Make an IRA (Individual Retirement Account) contribution You won't be required to pay taxes on the money you deposit to a standard IRA until you take it out in retirement. The withdrawal age is seventy-two.

Make a contribution to a Roth IRA.

The money you donate to a Roth IRA is subject to taxation now, but you won't be responsible for paying taxes on it when you take it out in retirement. The withdrawal age is fifty-nine and fifty-five.

As an instance, if you contribute $10,000 to your IRA as an employee in the 24 percent tax rate, you will avoid paying $2,400 in income tax that year.

Participate in an HSA

One of the easiest strategies for American taxpayers to minimize their retirement savings is to fund a Health Savings Account (HSA). A health savings account (HSA) offers tax advantages and can be utilized to cover eligible medical costs, such as insurance premiums. Since pre-tax income is required to be contributed to an HSA, your taxable income is decreased. Additionally, withdrawals from your HSA are tax-free provided you utilize the funds for approved medical costs. There are some considerations to make if you're considering making a donation to an HSA:

To be qualified for an HSA, you must first enroll in a high-deductible health insurance plan (HDHP).

Second, HSA contributions are limited. The freelancer's contribution cap for 2023 is $3,850 if they have self-only HDHP coverage; freelancers with family HDHP coverage can contribute up to $7,750.

Lastly, when you start an HSA account, you will need to choose a beneficiary.

Make a charitable donation

Giving to charities is one of the most well-liked methods for lawfully avoiding paying taxes. As a freelancer, you can lower your taxable income by donating to a private foundation or registered charity. You can also receive a tax receipt for your donation.

There are a few considerations to make sure you optimize your tax savings when you make charitable contributions:

Verify that the charity to which you are contributing is registered. The website of the tax authority in your nation allows you to confirm if a charity is registered.

The Internal Revenue Service in the US (irs.gov) or the UK (gov.uk) would be considered a tax authority.

Maintain a record of every gift you make so you can provide your receipts when asked.

To get the most advantage from your donations, make sure to declare them when submitting your taxes. Giving to charities helps individuals in need financially and is also a fantastic method to reduce taxed income.

While giving to charities usually doesn't result in financial savings, many of us value having more influence over the distribution of our taxed (or non-taxed) income.

Make a Child Tax Credit claim

A tax credit known as the Child Tax Credit is available to parents who file taxes and who have dependent children under the age of seventeen, there is a tax credit called the Child Tax Credit. Each child is eligible for a refundable tax credit of up to $2,000, which can be claimed each year when filing taxes.

Parents' gross income must be less than $200,000 for single parents and $400,000 for cohabiting parents in order to be eligible for the maximum tax credit. Every youngster needs a current Social Security number. Furthermore, for more than half of the tax year, the child needs to live with the taxpayer.

Chapter 9

Wise management of time

Time management is the process of allocating a certain amount of time to each task. Effective time management reduces stress, makes it possible to accomplish more in less time, and promotes job success. Many people question why it's important to consider our financial situation. Even if it seems like a nuisance or expense, dedicating an hour of your week to your money can yield substantial returns on investment (ROI) and benefit you for many generations to come. There will be financial, psychological, and emotional outcomes, among others. Invest sensibly by making financial and personal investments in yourself.

Time Management Strategies to Increase Your Income

The proverb "time is money" is not simply a catchy saying; it's a fact that the two are more closely related than you may imagine. Individuals who have mastered time management techniques typically report higher levels of productivity, which translates into more effective planning and revenue generation.

"I leveraged my time management skills to secure a promotion," stated DealNews.com consumer researcher Michael Bonebright. Spreadsheets and email were the former methods of handling workflow in our department. For me, this was completely ineffective, therefore I suggested moving to productivity software. Upon my boss's approval, I was tasked with locating the software and subsequently integrating the team.

I was in a position to take over when my boss left to work for another company.

Though this is obviously an extreme situation, it can be very beneficial to demonstrate to superiors that you are concerned about output. However, you can't assist others if you don't first manage your own time well.

Effective time management requires more than just using apps and other services. Additionally, it's a psychological encounter. A variety of financial experts were approached by GOBankingRates in order to acquire time management techniques that would increase your income.

1. Clearly State Your Financial Objectives

As stated by Bonebright, there are numerous benefits to improving your time management. Money can be one advantage. But first, you need a solid plan in order to apply effective time management to finances. This entails understanding your objectives, as MeMoreMoney creator and personal finance expert Mary Elizabeth noted. You'll save money in the long run if you are clear about what you want to achieve in the end.

Elizabeth advised, "Sit down and set what your financial goals are, then write them down." Ask yourself where you hope to be financially in a year, five years, and ten years. Subsequently, compute the appropriate budget amounts and devise a management strategy.

2. Establish Your Own Hourly Rate

The CEO of Best of Budgets and licensed financial counselor George Guillelmina said, "You still earn a certain amount of money per year regardless of whether you are employed, run your own business, or are a passive investor." As such, you are able to calculate your hourly rate.

Making hourly rate your own compass to help you become a more capable decision maker is the aim.

3. Take a seat comfortably Say No, and Stand Up (Literally)

Chris Taylor, marketing director at Profit Guru, stated, "The difference between fruitful individuals and extremely effective individuals is that exceptionally effective individuals say 'no' to nearly everything." He also suggested, if possible, standing up more during meetings.

Taylor advised, "Direct your gatherings standing up." I find it to be a quicker way to be serious, make a decision, and take care of things. When I get the chance, I usually like to take things a step further by holding a mobile meeting. Have time to ponder: Rather than chatting on the phone or going to events, I make an effort to think a lot and to spend more time thinking about things. Put another way, wherever feasible, stop sending back and forth emails.

4. Wisely Handle Stress

According to Julian Goldie, CEO of Goldie Agency, "stress often transpires when we accept more work than we are proficient in succeeding." The inference is that fatigue is a response that our bodies have, and it can affect our output. Although everyone experiences stress differently, there are several effective strategies to manage it, such as working out, meditating, listening to music, engaging in your favorite pastime, talking to friends, going outside, or listening to podcasts.

5. Strictly Limit Your Social Media Time

"As a result of COVID-19, many of my employees are having trouble managing their time," stated Daniel Foley, the creator of a digital marketing firm. "I would be lying if I said it didn't have some effect on the business overall, but we are being forgiving of them because it is really scary."

According to Foley, employees who work from home are not under supervision, which means they may be doing other things. It is difficult to work while your subconscious tells you that you are at home, therefore this makes sense, according to Foley.

The occasional five-minute per hour social media scroll is usually not too much of a time waste, but individuals who become completely engrossed in the activity can run into problems.

We've all experienced muscle memory gone wrong when we open the Facebook app after closing it, but this may be troublesome. Even if it might only be two minutes occasionally, the time adds up. When you're at home, I strongly suggest that you either follow a routine or, if you live with others, ask them to let you know if they see you slack off. It's normal for us to do so, but learn to stop yourself from doing it.

6. Establish deadlines

Goldie advised, "When you have a task at hand, set a reasonable deadline and stick to it." Once a deadline has been set, it could be crucial to write it down and place it close to your desk on a sticky note. This will provide you with an obvious signal to focus. In order to complete all the tasks that can get in the way, try to establish a deadline a few days before the assignment is due. Take stock of yourself and meet the deadline. Give yourself a reward when you complete a challenging task on your to-do list quickly.

7. Don't Waste Time Stressing Over Small Things

According to Akua Sarhene of Dem Coins Finance, "allocating your time and energy properly is the best time management skill that I have found." "Stop wasting so much time arguing over insignificant issues.

Save your energy and stop fretting if you should move your savings account because the interest rate went from 1.00% to.70%. Savings accounts aren't meant to make you wealthy, and the annual difference of.30% is hardly noticeable."

8. Let Go of Perfection

"Finishing a project is better than making it perfect' is the best time management tip we have found that saves resources across the organization," stated Jenna Carsom, Music Grotto's HR director.

There internal investigation revealed that some departments inside the company dedicated more than half of their project duration to perfecting the smallest things instead of producing outcomes that truly mattered. Certain projects will always require more attention than others, but if you're a competent leader, your work should be done well before focusing too much on the minor details.

9. Set a timer for productivity

According to Score Sense founder John Davis, "it is financially beneficial to finish tasks in the shortest possible time if you are paid on completion of them." "The amount of time we lose during the day juggling different jobs is staggering. By using a productivity meter such as Hub-staff, you can see how many hours you really work and identify places where you can cut down on time wastage.

10. Unwind!

Relaxing is one time-management strategy that can help you save money, according to Tax Hub creator and C.P.A. George Birrell. Yes, I realize that sounds counterproductive, but bear with me: Being "on the go" all the time is one of the issues that many individuals these days face. Your brain never gets a break when you're working on something and always thinking about what to do next. This can lead to subpar performance, financial results, and other outcomes.

You can benefit much from setting aside time during the day to unwind, even if it's only for half an hour or an hour. If you follow through on this, you should be able to return to your work with a clear head and be able to manage your finances more effectively, potentially saving a good amount of money and making wiser judgments.

The advantages of devoting time to your finances

The best investment is knowledge, which produces the biggest returns. Benjamin Franklin Invest sensibly by making financial and personal investments in yourself. It's critical to have good time management and investment skills. Effective time management promotes increased productivity and efficiency, reduced stress, and more success in life. Here are a few advantages of time management and investment into your finances:

1. Financial Stability: You can attain more financial stability by investing time in managing your finances. This include making a budget, keeping tabs on your spending, and making future plans. Knowing exactly where you stand financially allows you to make wise choices that bring security and stability.

2. Increased money: Over time, you can build money by practicing sound financial management. Through diligently tracking your earnings, outlays, and investments, you may pinpoint opportunities for enhancement and execute calculated choices that augment your total assets. This can entail increasing savings, making prudent investments, and looking into other sources of income.

3. Less Stress: Managing your money well can help you feel less stressed about it. With a sound financial strategy in place, you can put an end to concerns regarding money and have peace of mind.

Your mental and emotional health will improve when you are able to manage unforeseen costs or crises without feeling overburdened by debt.

4. Independence and Freedom: You might feel independent and free from financial constraints if you manage your money well.

You become less dependent on other people for financial support when you are in charge of your financial circumstances. This gives you the freedom to make decisions that support your objectives and moral principles, whether that means launching a business, going back to school, or taking a leave of absence to travel.

5. More Effective Relationships: Having sound financial management and stability can have a good relationship-building effect. Stress and disagreements about money are frequent causes of conflict in partnerships. Time well spent on finances can improve teamwork and communication with your company partners, family, and partners, leading to happier and healthier relationships.

6. Benefits to Future Generations: You help future generations as well as yourself by handling your money sensibly. You may teach your kids and other loved ones priceless lessons and resources by building a solid financial foundation. This can be giving them financial education, leaving them an inheritance, or sponsoring opportunities for them to pursue successful education.

7. Adaptability and Prospects: Good money management makes life more flexible and opens doors to new opportunities. Having your finances in order allows you to take advantage of possibilities to grow personally or establish a business or invest in real estate. Having financial stability gives you the freedom to try new things and take measured chances, which improves your quality of life in general. Time spent on finances is time invested in the future and in you.

Consequences of Ineffective Time Management

Let's also discuss the drawbacks of inadequate time management.

1. Ineffective workflow

Poor efficiency is the result of not being able to set goals and make advance plans. For instance, if there are multiple crucial chores to finish, a good strategy would be to complete related tasks together or sequentially. But if you don't make a strategy, you can find yourself needing to go back and forth, or backtrack, while working. This results in decreased production and efficiency.

2. Time lost

Time is lost as a result of poor time management. For example, when you use social media to talk with friends while working on an assignment, you are squandering time and diverting your attention.

3. A loss of command

You experience a lack of control over your life when you are unsure of what has to be done next. That may be a factor in increased worry and stress.

4. Subpar output

Your job will usually suffer in quality if you have poor time management skills. For instance, rushing to finish assignments at the last minute typically results in a compromise in quality.

5. A negative perception

If you are not dependable in completing tasks on time, it affects the expectations and perceptions of your clients as well as your company. A client will probably go elsewhere if they can't count on you to complete an assignment on time.

Chapter 10

Checklist for Financial Freedom

What Is Financial Freedom?

For most people, achieving financial freedom is their goal. Having enough cash on hand, investments, and savings to support the lifestyle we want for our kids and ourselves is typically a prerequisite for being **financially free**. It entails building up savings so we can pursue our desired careers or retire without feeling pressured to meet annual income requirements. When we are financially free, our money works for us instead of against us.

How may one achieve financial independence?

While some of the things on this list are straightforward activities that you can complete in a day, others are important issues that will require some time to resolve. Because each person's circumstances are distinct and diverse, some of them will apply to your scenario while others won't, which is why personal finance is referred to as such. There won't be a single, identical strategy used by two people to achieve financial independence.

There is no specific order in which this checklist is written. So, browse through the list in its whole and begin where it most convenient for you. Some of these problems could already be under control and you can cross them off right now. As many as possible that apply to you, good luck!

Assist periodically

Begin contributing on a regular basis. When you do, the sow/reap process and the Law of Attraction will come into play. Your concern of running out of money will start to fade as you soon realize that you harvest what you sow, so you can put your anxiety of running out of money aside.

Cuts your expenses

Reducing as much of your expenses as you can is one of the simplest strategies to gain control over your money and pay off debt rapidly. It's not that difficult if you're really dedicated. Because we don't know what we spend our money on, we usually waste significantly more than we realize. Reviewing ALL of your expenses when you sit down can help you identify areas where you can start making savings.

Use less than you generate

If you commit to doing just one simple step, you might potentially toss out the checklist and never have to worry about your financial freedom again. Building money and achieving financial freedom requires spending less than you earn. It is the most crucial problem that you should solve and become an expert at. Even if you complete every other action on the checklist, you won't achieve financial freedom until you control your spending. If you spend more than you earn, You will struggle or possibly go bankrupt if you neglect this one fundamental guideline, regardless of your income and salary.

Eliminate debt

The most thrilling and exhilarating sensation is being free of debt. Just stick to your offensive strategy. If you want to expedite the process of paying off your debt, the snowball method is the most effective approach. Ask for a lower rate on your credit cards. Give your creditor enough time to negotiate a lower interest rate. Call your creditors frequently while you are in a serious payback mood, and occasionally hang up to negotiate a better interest rate. At the very least, it's worth the time to ask.

Creation and aid fund

This is common knowledge, and having an emergency fund on hand will help you avoid debt and be able to deal with life's challenges.

Get rid of your junk

Want to pay off debt with cash? Trade in your clutter. Many of us live in homes that are overly cluttered. Sell what you can through consignment, Facebook Marketplace, or yard sales. Take that money and use every last cent to pay down your debt. Put that money into your emergency fund if you're debt-free! Form a spending guide. Making a monthly spending plan guarantees that you are allocating your funds wisely and are not "hoping for the best" or squandering them.

You can use an online service like Mint, make your own template in an Excel spreadsheet, or download one of our many free budgeting forms. The important thing is that you do it; how you do it is irrelevant.

Get your 401(k) with the employer match

Speaking with someone who is a few years behind retirement will come up unexpectedly, and if you're not ready, you could get into a big problem. Make the most of any matching benefits offered by your employer. You'd be a fool not to take advantage of the simplest method available to increase your retirement savings—it's almost free money.

Monitor your spending

Although it is a task that no one enjoys, tracking your expenditures is the greatest way to get a clear picture of where your money is going when you're first starting out. You'll be able to better manage your expenditure by doing this and find costs that you can reduce.

Set your bank accounts up

Do yourself a favor and take the time to arrange your bank accounts, track deposits and withdrawals, and balance your account each month if your finances are a complete disaster. Perhaps having multiple accounts can help you overcome your disarray. You can use this helpful method to help you achieve your financial freedom goals by keeping several accounts for different purposes.

Set goals for your career and earnings

It's possible that your current activities aren't enabling you to make as much money as you could. If so, you might want to think about switching jobs or careers in order to advance and achieve financial independence. Think of becoming your own boss or launching a blog.

Assess your needs for a car

The majority of Americans overpay for their cars. Consider your family's needs in this regard and make any necessary cuts. Instead of having an endless auto loan, trade in a less expensive model and begin paying cash for your car.

Eliminate as much tax as possible

To be sure you're taking all the allowable and legitimate deductions, you can work with a tax accountant. Paying more in taxes than necessary is absurd when you have to labor 107 days a year to meet the demands of the government.

Discover your essential periods

Many of us have a problem with emotional spending, which leads to massive debt. Your financial future will thank you if you can identify what your money triggers are, what you're attempting to replace shopping for, and then replace that need with something healthy and less expensive.

Determine your net worth

Your existing financial situation will become clearer when you calculate your net worth. The difference between the total value of your assets and the total amount of debt you have outstanding is your net worth.

Buy only the things you need

The masses are confused by consumerism. They consequently experience "consumer confusion." They have lost the ability to distinguish between needs and wants. Once you understand the differences, resolve to buy needs exclusively.

Streamline the process of paying bills

Try automating if you can. Long-term, it will make things easier for you. Just make sure you have enough cash on hand to pay all of your expenses that are deducted from your income automatically to avoid paying hefty fees.

Determine your actual hourly wage

This is a great method to help you determine the value of your time and whether your current employment is worthwhile.

Seek appropriate insurance

Some people should obtain life insurance; for example, if you have children who are not yet adults, you should. But what about adequate house and auto insurance and disability insurance? Health-related? More quickly than anything else, illness and accidents will disrupt your financial ambitions.

Take a seat with a reliable and trustworthy insurance broker and go over everything to make sure you have the right coverage for your particular situation.

Use money

Start managing your money and income with cash and the cash envelope technique if you're having trouble with debt and overspending. It will significantly alter the way you view money and assist you in controlling your expenditure.

Develop a system for keeping financial records

Would your family know where to retrieve your financial records if you passed away tomorrow? Would they make sense and be in order? If not, do your loved ones a favor and organize your financial records into a smanageable structure that they can access.

Conclusion

Anyone, not just the wealthy or those with expertise in finance, has to possess this essential skill set of financial intelligence. You can live a more secure and satisfying life by using it to help you make wiser financial decisions. Budgeting, saving, investing, controlling debt, financial planning, and risk management are only a few of the core concepts of financial knowledge that are necessary for financial intelligence. Adding these components to your daily life may take time and effort, but the effort will eventually pay off.

Financial intelligence leads to financial intelligence behaviors such as creating a positive financial mindset, working for yourself for at least two hours after working for someone else for eight hours, expert budgeting, financial leveraging, automating financial decisions, calculating your net worth, avoiding needless taxes, and wise management of time.

Sound financial intelligence is built on a positive financial mindset. A positive financial attitude is a collection of upbeat thoughts and perspectives about money that guide choices for budgeting, saving, and distribution. A strong and fully positive financial mindset inspires you to plan for eventual financial independence and freedom by igniting your enthusiasm for money. These strategies include creating a budget, carving out at least an extra two hours each day for personal time, accumulating savings, bringing in extra cash, and selecting prudent investments.

There are several reasons why financial intelligence is important. It raises people's standard of living and aids in financial management. As such, financial intelligence is an essential component of our lives that necessitates thoughtful consideration and preparation.

People can attain financial security and stability by making an informed budget, saving and investing sensibly, and using their time appropriately. It's also critical to educate oneself on financial concepts and to regularly review and modify strategies and a financial independence checklist in response to changing circumstances. We can work toward financial freedom and provide the foundation for a stable financial future by taking charge of our finances.

REFERENCES

Active Wealth, (2023). HOW TO AVOID UNNECESSARY TAX BURDENS https://www.activatewealthllc.com/2020/05/13/how-to-avoid-unnecessary-tax-burdens/ (Accessed 11th January, 2024).

Adam Haye, (2023). What Is Financial Leverage, and Why Is It Important? https://www.investopedia.com/terms/l/leverage.asp (Accessed 11th January, 2024).

AKHILESH GANTI, (2023). Net Worth: What It Is and How to Calculate It. https://www.investopedia.com/terms/n/networth.asp (Accessed 11th January, 2024).

Alexandre Negredo, (2021). The 7 Habits of Financial Intelligence: An easy guide with the money mindset to achieve your financial freedom. https://www.amazon.com/gp/aw/d/B09KBTD4PS/ref=tmm_kin_swatch_0?ie=UTF8&qid=1704747408&sr=8-14 (Accessed 8th January, 2024).

Anonymous, (2019). 10 Reasons why financial intelligent is the key to success. https://opportunitydesk.org/2019/01/25/10-reasons-why-financial-intelligence-is-a-key-to-success/ (Accessed 3rd January, 2024).

Baba Sadar, (2023). 12 Tips To Develop Financial Intelligence. https://medium.com/@babasadar/12-tips-to-develop-financial-intelligence-d2c0e94a95cb (Accessed 8th January, 2024).

Cave Financial, (2023). 7 Benefits Of Investing Time Into Your Finances. https://cavefinancial.co.nz/blog/150/7-benefits-of-investing-time-into-your-finances/ (Accessed 12th January, 2024).

CFI Team, (2024). Time Management: Planning and controlling how much time to spend on specific activities. https://corporatefinanceinstitute.com/resources/management/time-management-list-tips/ (Accessed 12th January, 2024).

CHARLIE GILKEY, (2013). Use the Two-Hour Rule to Make Progress on Your Creative Projects. https://www.productiveflourishing.com/p/the-two-hour-rule (Accessed 13th January, 2024).

DRS, (2023). What is Financial Freedom? Practical steps on how you can become financially free. https://www.moneyfit.org/financial-freedom-means/ (Accessed 28th January, 2024).

Fastal Capital, (2023). Ways to Automate Your Finances and Save Money https://fastercapital.com/content/Ways-to-Automate-Your-Finances-and-Save-Money.html (Accessed 11th January, 2024).

Felix Akinnibi, (2023). What is Financial Intelligence? https://cowrywise.com/blog/financial-intelligence/ (Accessed 3rd January, 2024).

Global Citizen Solution, (2023). How to Avoid Paying Taxes Legally: A Detailed Guide. https://www.globalcitizensolutions.com/how-to-avoid-paying-taxes-legally/ (Accessed 22th January, 2024).

Ingressive for Good, (2023). How To Build A Positive Money Mindset. https://ingressive.org/how-to-build-a-positive-money-mindset/ (Accessed 16th February, 2024).

Katie Byrne, (2022). How to budget like a pro. https://m.independent.ie/business/personal-finance/how-to-budget-like-a-pro/41241303.html (Accessed 11th January, 2024).

Larry E. Kinsey and Bartholomew O. Utazi, (2024). Personal Finance: Easy Approaches to Complete Financial Control, Financial Independence, and Early Retirement. https://www.amazon.com/PERSONAL-FINANCE-Approaches-Independence-Retirement/dp/B0CV4CH8K7 (Accessed 15th March, 2024).

MAUREEN CAMPAIOLA, (2024). MY FINANCIAL FREEDOM CHECKLIST. https://adebtfreestressfreelife.com/financial-freedom-checklist/ ,(Accessed 13th January, 2024).

Nicole Spector, (2021)· 10 Time Management Tips That Can Help You Make More Money. https://finance.yahoo.com/news/10-time-management-tips-help-163600532.html (Accessed 12th January, 2024).

Olayemi Oni, (2023). Financial Intelligence: What you should know. https://bitnob.com/blog/financial-intelligence-what-you-should-know (Accessed 8th January, 2024).

Ramsey, (2023). What Is Your Net Worth? https://www.ramseysolutions.com/retirement/what-is-your-net-worth (Accessed 11th January, 2024).

Reaprite, (2023). PERSONAL FINANCE; How To Develop Financial Intelligence. https://blog.reaprite.com/how-to-develop-financial-intelligence/ (Accessed 8th January, 2024).

Rinse Team, (2024). How To Get An Extra 2 Hours In A Day. https://www.rinse.com/blog/life/how-to-get-an-extra-2-hours-in-a-day/ (Accessed 13th January, 2024).

Sam, (2023). Set It and Forget It: 11 Easy Ways to Automate Your Finances. https://www.smarterandharder.com/financial-automation/ (Accessed 11th January, 2024).

www.ingramcontent.com/pod-product-compliance
Lightning Source LLC
Chambersburg PA
CBHW062117220526
45471CB00010B/3770